FANDOM FEVER

THE BTS ARMY

BY VIRGINIA LOH-HAGAN

45TH PARALLEL PRESS

Published in the United States of America by
Cherry Lake Publishing Group
Ann Arbor, Michigan
www.cherrylakepublishing.com

Reading Adviser: Beth Walker Gambro, MS, Ed., Reading Consultant, Yorkville, IL
Content Advisers: Elisabeth Oakes and Brooklyn Blevins
Book Designer: Joseph Hatch

Photo Credits: © SOPA Images Limited/Alamy Stock Photo, cover, title page; Divine
Treasure, CC BY 4.0 via Wikimedia Commons, 4; © Joietotheworld/Shutterstock, 7;
© Everything You Need/Shutterstock, 8; mduangdara, CC BY 2.0 via Wikimedia
Commons, 11; Senate Democrats, CC BY 2.0 via Wikimedia Commons, 12; © lev radin/
Shutterstock, 13; HopeSmiling, CC BY 4.0 via Wikimedia Commons, 14; © NRien/
Shutterstock, 17; © Salsabila Azkya/Shutterstock, 19; © Sipa USA/Alamy Stock Photo, 21;
© Naumova Ekaterina/Shutterstock, 22; © MediaPunch Inc/Alamy Stock Photo, 25;
© Dutchmen Photography/Shutterstock, 26; © Sam the Leigh/Shutterstock, 29;
© Naumova Ekaterina/Shutterstock

Copyright © 2025 by Cherry Lake Publishing Group

All rights reserved. No part of this book may be reproduced or utilized in any form or
by any means without written permission from the publisher.

45th Parallel Press is an imprint of Cherry Lake Publishing Group.

Library of Congress Cataloging-in-Publication Data

Names: Loh-Hagan, Virginia, author.
Title: The BTS ARMY / Virginia Loh-Hagan.
Description: Ann Arbor : 45th Parallel Press, 2024. | Series: Fandom fever | Audience:
   Grades 4-6 | Summary: "The BTS ARMY provides an inside look at the powerful
   fandom of BTS. Readers will get hooked on this hi-lo title, covering facts about and
   insights into the group of fans who aren't afraid to make their support of this K-pop
   boy band known"— Provided by publisher.
Identifiers: LCCN 2024009622 | ISBN 9781668947494 (hardcover) | ISBN 9781668948880
   (paperback) | ISBN 9781668950401 (ebook) | ISBN 9781668954966 (pdf)
Subjects: LCSH: BTS (Musical group)—Juvenile literature. | Popular music fans—Juvenile
   literature.
Classification: LCC ML3930.B89 L65 2024 | DDC 781.630922—dc23/eng/20240227
LC record available at https://lccn.loc.gov/2024009622

Cherry Lake Publishing Group would like to acknowledge the work of the Partnership for
21st Century Learning, a Network of Battelle for Kids. Please visit Battelle for Kids online
for more information.

Note from publisher: Websites change regularly, and their future contents are outside
of our control. Supervise children when conducting any recommended online searches
for extended learning opportunities.

Printed in the United States of America

Table of Contents

CHAPTER ONE
From Fan Base to Fandom 5

CHAPTER TWO
Fanning BTS 9

CHAPTER THREE
Living That Fan Life 15

CHAPTER FOUR
The Power of Fandom 20

CHAPTER FIVE
Insider Information 24

Glossary 32

Learn More 32

Index 32

Dr. Virginia Loh-Hagan is an author and educator. She is currently the Director of the Asian Pacific Islander Desi American (APIDA) Center at San Diego State University and the Co-Executive Director of The Asian American Education Project. She lives in San Diego with her very tall husband and very naughty dogs.

BTS members hug. They had just won an Artist of the Year award.

CHAPTER ONE

From Fan Base to Fandom

Musicians make music. They perform music. Some become big stars. They become **celebrities**. Celebrities are famous. They have a **fan base**. A fan base is a group of supporters.

Most fans have a casual interest. But some fans are more devoted. They worship their **idols**. Idols are big stars. Devoted fans form **fandoms**. Fandoms are communities. They're networks of fans.

Fandoms of musicians are special groups. They buy the musicians' music. They buy their **merch**. Merch means merchandise. It means stuff that can be sold. Merch includes shirts and posters. Fans follow musicians on tour. They attend their shows. They go on tour with them. They connect with the music. They connect with the messages. They sing their songs. They know all the words.

Fandoms are a powerful force. They can influence music. They use the internet. The internet gives fans information about their idols. It gives them more access to their idols. It also gives them more access to other fans.

Fans build relationships with each other. They share their knowledge. They share their passion. They build connections. They create content. They share content.

Fans make fan art. This is when they draw pictures of their idols. Fans also write stories about their idols. This is called fan fiction. They share their art. They share their stories.

Some celebrities have large fandoms. Their fandoms even have special names. That's a sign of success!

There is a wide range of BTS fan art posted online.

The "Korean wave" is the global interest in South Korean pop culture. It started in the 1990s. There is a lot of K-pop merch. There are even BTS dolls!

CHAPTER TWO

Fanning BTS

BTS is a South Korean boy band. BTS stands for *Bangtan Sonyeondan*. This means "Bulletproof Boy Scouts" in Korean. The band aims to block out negative thoughts about teens. BTS songs try to empower young people. They arm fans with strength. In 2017, BTS changed their image. They said their name stands for "Beyond The Scene." They wanted to move from being kids to adults.

BTS formed in 2010. Today, there's great interest in South Korean pop music. This is known as **K-pop**.

The band members are RM, Jin, SUGA, j-hope, Jimin, V, and Jungkook. They started as a hip-hop group. They expanded. Now they perform many music styles.

BTS songs are top hits. The band performs all around the world. Their shows sell out. They always have big crowds. They have sold many albums. They have won many awards. They're loved by many. Their fandom is known as ARMY.

ARMY stands for Adorable Representative M.C. for Youth. M.C. stands for master of ceremonies. A master of ceremonies is a host. They speak for others. In this way, BTS fans speak for youth. They feel pressured by their parents and society. They want to live their own dreams.

ARMY is inspired by BTS songs. BTS songs are about youth issues. They address mental health. They address teen troubles. They address self-love. They address real topics. These topics matter to their fans.

The BTS fandom was almost named The Bells. *Bang* sounds like *bell* in Korean. Bells also make noise. And BTS wanted to "make some noise."

SUPER FAN

Mazie Hirono is a big BTS fan. She was born in 1947. She's a U.S. senator. She represents Hawai'i. She's the first elected female senator from Hawai'i. She's the first Asian American female senator. She's the first U.S. senator born in Japan. She's the first **Buddhist** senator. She supports racial justice. She helped pass the COVID-19 Hate Crimes bill. She did this in 2021. She wants to end anti-Asian hate. She shares that goal with BTS. She said, "...I love BTS. And I'm proud of it." Her favorite song is "Permission to Dance." She said, "It really makes me proud and happy that a group from South Korea can have this very positive impact. Because if you listen to any of their songs, it is about being yourself, loving yourself." When BTS went to the White House, Hirono tweeted. She wrote, "I'm the only U.S. Senator who knows who BTS is."

ARMY also refers to a military army. Fans are the army. And BTS is the armor. Armor protects the army. This means BTS and their fans are always together. BTS shows their fans love. They write songs telling ARMY they'll be there for them.

ARMY is very organized. They have hosted many fan projects. Fan projects help fans be seen. Fans organize projects before shows. They go into action during shows. An example is making signs. ARMY often has pictures of BTS band members' faces. They also host contests.

ARMY does things for BTS. ARMY donates to BTS's causes. They follow their social media. They push to feature BTS on radio and TV.

"2!3!" is a BTS song. It encourages ARMY to let go of bad memories. It tells them to make new memories together with BTS and other fans.

BTS band members often use purple hearts in their social media. They want to promote love.

CHAPTER THREE

Living That Fan Life

ARMY shows up at BTS events. To be ARMY, make sure to look the part! Do the following:

+ Wear purple. Purple means love. It means trust. Say, "I purple you."

+ Bring ARMY Bombs. These are light sticks. They sync with the music. They change colors. They enhance the show experience.

+ Get BTS merch. Fans have created lots of BTS stuff. These include stickers and pins. ARMY also wears shirts from other shows.

+ Style yourself after your favorite BTS song. Examples are "DNA" or "IDOL." These songs have lots of energy. Wear bright colors!

ARMY has their own culture. To be ARMY, make sure to act the part! Do the following:

+ Host or go to a **cupsleeve** event. Cupsleeves wrap around cups. Fans meet in cafes. They get free cupsleeves for buying drinks. There's a limited number of designs. ARMY collects the cup sleeves.

+ Participate in BTS Island: In the SEOM. BTS Island: In the SEOM is a video game.

+ Learn BTS dance moves. Make dance videos. BTS is known for their creative dancing. ARMY loves to copy them.

+ Get ready for Random Play Dance. These events feature BTS songs. They are played back-to-back. Fans listen. If they know the song, they act. They dance. They sing.

There was even a McDonald's BTS meal.

Fanatic Fan

South Korean men ages 18 to 28 are required to do military service. They must enlist in the military for 18 to 21 months. The term length depends on the branch of the military. A special law was passed for K-pop stars. K-pop stars could delay joining until age 30. In 2022, Jin was the first to enlist. He's the oldest. By 2023, the others enlisted. They had to take a break from music. K-pop brings a lot of money to South Korea. Some ARMY fans are organizing boycotts. They want people to stop supporting K-pop until BTS returns. A fan said, "I am a fan of BTS. And I am not a fan of the Korean government. They must realize what they have done." Another fan said, "I won't buy anything until the boys are back." Lee "Faker" Sang-hyeok is a video game star. He's famous. He's won gold medals. He beat China at the 2023 Asian Games. He was allowed to skip military service. This angered ARMY. ARMY attacked Faker. They begged for BTS to also be excused.

Not all fan behavior is good. Some fans can be **toxic**. Toxic means harmful. In Korea, toxic fans are called **sasaeng**. To be ARMY, don't let your passion become poison. Do the following:

+ Respect BTS's privacy. Toxic fans have stalked them. They've broken into their hotel rooms.

+ Don't be mean to other fans. Some fans have started fan wars. They say mean things about other K-pop groups. They say mean things about other K-pop fandoms.

+ Don't pit band members against each other. Fans often like one member more than others. But all the band members are special.

People have a right to live their lives. Focus on the art more than the artist.

Be a fun fan! Get together with other BTS fans for shows and events.

CHAPTER FOUR

The Power of Fandom

ARMY is inspired by BTS. They support them. They support their causes. Together, they're a powerful force. They've helped people. They've made social changes.

In 2017, BTS helped launch "Love Myself." This program aimed to end violence against young people. BTS donated money. They talked to world leaders. They made a music video about love and kindness. They said, "We started Love Myself as a way to reach young people and help improve their lives and rights… We will be honored if all seven of us can continue this campaign to return the amazing love that we have received…"

This inspired many fans to launch their own **charities**. Charities raise money. They help those in need. Some created One In An Army. The motto is "I am ONE in an ARMY." They believe many people giving small amounts can create a big impact.

ARMY translates songs. Translate means to explain in different languages. ARMY wants everyone to have access to BTS's words.

BTS stood with Black Lives Matter. This happened in 2020. BTS helped support racial justice. They donated 1 million dollars. ARMY matched this. They raised more than 1 million dollars in a few days. They used **hashtag activism**. This is the use of hashtags on social media. Hashtags note topics on social media. They help build public support.

People protested for Black Lives Matter in Dallas, Texas. The Dallas police asked people to send them videos. They wanted people to snitch on protestors. The fan community thought this was wrong. K-pop fans urged other K-pop fans to flood the site with other content.

ARMY flooded snitch apps with cute pictures. They posted their favorite K-pop artists.

Idol Inspiration

Idols have idols. RM is the leader of BTS. He's a rapper. He's a big fan of Drake. Drake was born in 1986. He's a Canadian rapper and actor. He's a top-selling artist. He sings about his feelings. He mixes singing and rapping. He inspired RM to start singing. He influenced RM's flow. In 2010, Drake released *Thank Me Later*. RM said, "That album was kind of shocking for me...it was kind of a freaky thing that a rapper actually sang. So after that, a lot of rappers began to sing..." RM said he "wanted to do something just like him." Other BTS members like Drake too. They met Drake in 2019. They met him at an awards show. ARMY fans also like Drake. They share pics of Drake in purple. They edit his clothing colors. They change them to purple. They change his skin to purple. They add BTS swag to his look.

CHAPTER FIVE

Insider Information

Fans know their idols. They can also spot fake fans. Make sure you do your research. Here are the top 10 things every true ARMY should know about BTS!

1. BTS was formed by Korea's Big Hit Entertainment. Singers **auditioned**. Auditions are tryouts. Big Hit chose members. BTS members trained for years. They **debuted** in 2013. Debut means to launch in public.

2. BTS's first single was "No More Dream." Their first full-length album was *Dark & Wild*. They topped the charts. And they kept doing it.

3. All ARMY should know the fan chant. List BTS members' names by age after the leader. "Kim Namjoon, Kim Seokjin, Min Yoongi, Jung Hoseok, Park Jimin, Kim Taehyung, Jeon Jungkook, BTS!"

BTS had different band name choices. Names included Big Kidz and Young Nation.

If ARMY was a real army, there'd be a ton of soldiers.

4. RM learned English from TV. He watched *Friends* (1994–2004). This show was popular. It was about 6 friends. The friends lived in New York City.

5. BTS members used to live together. They shared one room. Then they moved to a bigger place. They split rooms. Now, they have their own homes. They live in a rich area in South Korea. Other South Korean stars live there too.

6. BTS members write many of their own songs. This is different from other boy bands. BTS likes trying different sounds. They aren't afraid of taking risks.

7. BTS members are also models. They have supported different brands. They promote fashion companies.

8. BTS went to the White House. They did this in 2022. They met U.S. President Joe Biden. They spoke against anti-Asian hate.

9. BTS has won hundreds of awards. They have set new records. They have also broken records. They have more than 23 world records. They're the most streamed group on Spotify. They have some of the most viewed YouTube videos.

10. BTS members have different hobbies. Jin likes fishing. He also plays video games. SUGA likes painting. He also likes working out. Jimin enjoys traveling and dancing. RM likes reading and visiting museums. V plays golf. Jungkook has a lot of hobbies. Making art and boxing are two of them. J-hope likes dance and photography.

There's so much more to learn! Make sure to keep up with the latest.

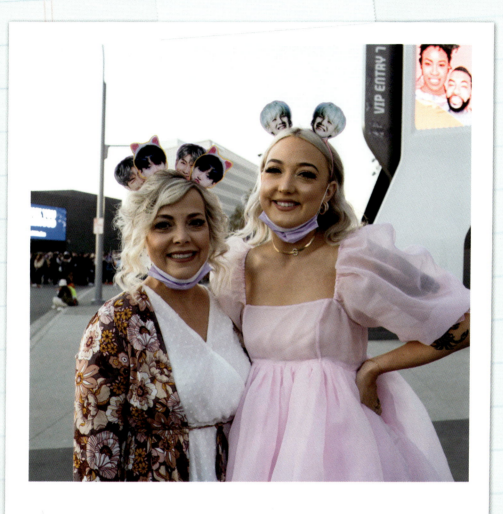

ARMY members like to dress up to go to BTS shows.

29

Fans have their own language. Here are some ARMY words you should know:

+ Apobangpo: This means "ARMY forever. Bangtan forever."

+ BANGTANTV: This YouTube channel shows BTS music videos. It has fun videos of their lives.

+ Bias: Bias means favorite. Most ARMY fans have a favorite band member.

+ Bias Wrecker: When another band member distracts fans from their bias.

+ *Bon Voyage*: BTS's reality show. It records their vacations. It records their adventures in different cities.

+ Borahae: This term combines two Korean words. *Bora* is violet. *Saranghae* means "I love you."

+ BT21: BT21 stands for BTS and 21st century. It's a branding company. They have cute products. Their products represent BTS members.

+ Festa: Festa celebrates the anniversary of BTS's debut. The debut date is June 13. Festa lasts more than a week.

+ Muster: A big show that ends Festa. Muster is a military word. It means to gather troops.

RM is the leader of BTS. RM used to stand for "Rap Monster." He changed it to just RM in 2017. His real name is Kim Nam-joon. He said, "I'm your fan, too. A fan who silently supports the loneliness, the battles, and the life you're going through. I send you my letters written with music and notes from behind the stage and at my studio. I hope you'll read the sounds that is me missing you."

There are all types of BTS fans. They're all around the world. Start your own fan club!

- Promote your fan club.
- Collect a list of names.
- Plan events.
- Host a meeting.
- Have fun!

Fans can buy special passes to BTS soundchecks.

GLOSSARY

auditioned (aw-DIH-shuhnd) tried out for a role or job by performing

Buddhist (BOO-dihst) someone who practices Buddhism, a religion from Asia, started in 6th century BCE by Buddha

celebrities (suh-LEH-bruh-teez) well-known or famous people

charities (CHAIR-uh-teez) organizations that raise money to help others

cupsleeve (KUHP-sleev) tube-shaped piece of material put on a cup for hot drinks

debuted (DAY-byood) made a first appearance

fan base (FAN BAYSS) group of fans for a particular sport, musical group, or celebrity

fandom (FAN-duhm) subculture, community, or network of fans who share a common interest

hashtag activism (HASH-tag AK-tih-vih-zuhm) use of hashtags to promote causes on social media

idols (EYE-duhlz) people who are greatly admired and loved by others

K-pop (KAY-pahp) South Korean popular culture, including music, movies, TV shows, fashion, and beauty products

merch (MURCH) short for merchandise, which includes posters, shirts, and other items

sasaeng (SAH-sang) South Korean term for an obsessive fan who invades the privacy of Korean idols

toxic (TAHK-sik) harmful

LEARN MORE

BTS: K-Pop Power! Carlton Books, 2020.

Kim, Yerin. *I Love BTS: An Unofficial Fan Journal.* New York, NY: Adams Media, 2023.

Wright, Becca. *BTS: Top of K-Pop.* London: Buster Books, 2023.

INDEX

awards, 4, 10, 28

Black Lives Matter, 22
BTS
   group biography, 9–10, 24–28
   photos, 4, 11, 14, 21, 22, 25

charitable giving, 20, 22
colors, 14, 15
concerts, 10, 11, 13, 25, 29
culture, 15–16, 30

dancing, 16
Drake, 23

famous fans, 12
fan art, 6, 7
fandoms, 5–6, 10, 13, 31

Hirono, Mazie, 12

j-hope, 7, 9, 11, 14, 24, 28
Jimin, 7, 8, 9, 11, 21, 24, 28
Jin, 7, 9, 11, 18, 24
Jungkook, 7, 9, 11, 22, 24, 28

K-pop, 8, 9, 18, 19

Lee "Faker" Sang-hyeok, 18
love and kindness, 20, 31

merchandise, 8, 15, 16
military service, 18

racial justice, 22
RM, 7, 9, 11, 23, 24, 27, 28, 31

social causes, 12, 20, 22, 28
social media, 14, 22
songs, 10, 12, 13, 15, 21, 24, 27
SUGA, 7, 9, 11, 24, 28

toxic behavior, 19
translations, 21

V, 7, 9, 11, 21, 24, 27, 28
vocabulary, 30